Coming Home:
an introduction
to the Quakers

Gerald Priestland

Quaker Books

2003

The content of this booklet is an edited version of an address given at Westminster Friends Meeting House, London, in May 1979, at a meeting arranged for people enquiring about the Religious Society of Friends. There have been some minor changes to the text since Gerald Priestland's death, with the permission of his widow.

First published 1981 by London & Middlesex General Meeting Extension Committee
Reprinted January 1983
October 1987
December 1993
by Quaker Home Service
This edition August 2003 by Quaker Books

ISBN 0 85245 349 3

Coming Home

George Fox was always a major stumbling block for me in the way of becoming a Quaker. There he was, this intolerant, self-made Mr Valiant-for-Truth, speaking in the Bible-prose of the English countryside, and walking boldly through the world 'gainst all disaster.

And then Fox's great message, that there is That of God in everyone, began to excite and illuminate me, and I saw that Quakerism – though Fox himself would have hated that sectarian term – is not just a mid 17th century aberration, but is for today, a day that longs for a poetic meaning to life but cannot accept it in the old metre.

What I want to do here is tell you something about the Religious Society of Friends; its origins and traditions, what it stands for – and in particular, what it means to me. If I tend to dwell on my own point of view, it is not because I am under any illusions as to my own importance or significance – to the Society or to anyone else – but for three other reasons.

First, since Quakers have no test of faith, or Creed, each of us can only speak for himself. No one person speaks for the Society; we have no Pope, no archbishop, no President or Moderator.

Secondly, Quakers have a distressingly virtuous reputation to live down – a reputation which, I suspect, actually discourages some people from joining us. Anyway, it can only be healthily undermined by putting up a gin-drinking hack journalist like me. If they will let me in, they will let anyone in. Maybe even you...

Thirdly, one remark of Fox's that clangs in my head like a bell. "Christ saith this, and the apostles say this – but what canst thou say?" In these matters nothing is valid, nothing counts, unless one knows it from one's own experience... and that lies at the heart of the Quaker vision.

*   *   *   *

My childhood background was Anglican; indeed, my paternal grandfather was an ordained minister of the Church of England and a preacher of some reputation and scholarship. I wish I had heard him, for sloppy sermons and too much mumbo jumbo drove me to the English Presbyterians, with whom I stayed for 20 years or so, much enjoying the metrical psalms.

But though the sermons were better, I became increasingly perplexed over the questions of Sin, Redemption, Atonement, Salvation, and indeed the whole meaning of the Passion and Crucifixion and Resurrection of Christ. That Christ was the most significant figure before me, I did not doubt, but what was that significance was, for me, became more obscure the more I listened to the ministers.

This became deeply troublesome to me, because in the course of my travels as a reporter, I was encountering a great deal of violence, in race riots, street crime, civil wars, and the battlegrounds of Vietnam and Ulster. The contemplation of it was oppressive.

4

Was the work I was doing useless, futile? My religion should have been able to confront that violence and make some sense out of life; but on the contrary, it only made me feel the more doomed and damned...

In part, of course, this was a personal neurotic problem, a typical case of depression, which came to a climax in a nervous breakdown. But as I lay on the psychiatrist's couch, listening to a classic Viennese accent helping me to disentangle things. I found that he was telling me – for a substantial fee every Tuesday morning – much the same things about human nature and the meaning of life that the Society of Friends was telling me free on Sundays.

That there was indeed That of Good (That of God) in everyone, including myself; that one should work to that, rather than the weak or corrupt side of our natures; and that our sins are forgiven – not will be, but are – if only we will forgive ourselves.

I had begun to attend Golders Green Meeting, and to write a book about the Problems of Violence. I realised that the problem of violence was not just in society, but in myself. I came to see violence as a form of communication to which people resort when the peaceful communication of language breaks down. In itself, I see violence as the supreme evil – the ultimate rejection of love. And so, to me, the Quaker stand against violence and war, George Fox's insistence on communicating with That of God in everyone, appeared as the most relevant expression of Christianity.

For me this is quite central to Quakerism. I experience Christ as the Christ of Non-Violence. His message (in my view) was that the Kingdom is upon us – is in us – now, and not some time yet to come; and that our sins are forgiven now.

Now this is clearly intolerable to any regime which has to depend upon guilt, fear and oppression. It was a revolutionary message. And because of the times he lived in, Christ was constantly assailed by attempts to politicise his mission – to turn it into what we would call a liberation movement. This made him still more of a troublemaker from the Establishment point of view. He was rocking the spiritual and political boat by his absolute refusal to compromise with the power, commercialism, cruelty and hypocrisy that stood in the way of his Kingdom.

The Agony in Gethsemane is the crucial point. If, there in the garden, Christ had decided to stand and fight, to join the Resistance Movement, or simply to run away, then Christianity would not have happened.

Christ chose to fight by surrendering; and though it shocks many of my Quaker friends when I say this, I find that moment far more important than the resurrection. For by choosing to die on the Cross – by the loving non-violence of his Passion – he turned evil into supreme good.

It is not that he just absorbed the evil by refusing bitterness and vengeance; by accepting death he finally ruled out any question of an earthly political kingdom and forced his followers into direct personal contact with the Spirit – which is the Light of God in all of us. This is how I see Christ, and you will soon understand that it is very much of a Quaker view.

To return to George Fox and the 17th century. It was the age of the Civil Wars; not only in England, but all over Europe, and for the most part they were wars of religion – the kind of wars that have rightly given religion a bad name. Almost everywhere, Church and State, Religion and Politics, were at stake side by side.

In England, Elizabeth the First had established a Calvinistic Protestant Church. You could, she allowed, believe anything you liked, provided you kept it to yourself and conformed to the Prayer Book in public – which meant acknowledging the doctrines of Original Sin, Justification by Faith, and the Sufficiency of the Holy Scripture for Salvation.

The fall of King Charles took the lid off all that; England heaved and seethed with all kinds of religious speculation from Anabaptism to Ranterism and the Fifth Monarchy Men. In due course, the Established Church and the Anglican Conformity were restored. But one of the most independent and remarkable groups to survive was the Society of Friends – called "Quakers" because, it was said, they quaked at the name of the Lord.

I think what really ensured the Quaker survival was that everyone else – High Church and Puritans alike – detested and persecuted them; and there is nothing like persecution to make a sect flourish.

At least 20,000 Friends were punished in one way or another for their faith; about 450 of them actually died in the squalor of prison. In North America, the Pilgrim Fathers, themselves refugees from European intolerance, publicly hanged four Quakers, one of them a woman.

Why? What was it all about? How did it all begin?

George Fox was the son of a pious Leicestershire weaver. By his own account, he was a fairly successful small-time cattle dealer. He was also, I fear a bit of a prig – he would not smoke or join a few friends in a modest drinking bout – and I would diagnose him as a fellow depressive. At any rate, he tells us "I was in great sorrows and troubles, and walked many nights by myself."

At the age of 19 he set out, wandering far and wide, listening to various notable Puritan preachers and teachers of the day, but getting no light or comfort from them at all. Gradually, after intensive reading of the Bible, various convictions began to take shape in his own mind.

First: that no amount of study at Oxford or Cambridge made a man into a priest.

Second: that God did not dwell in temples made with hands.

Third: that the Holy Scriptures themselves were dead without the Spirit.

And fourth: that the true meaning of the gospel had been lost and forgotten, and that the churches had been responsible for a great apostasy from the original faith of the apostles (this belief is not uncommon among reformers to this day).

So no wonder there was nobody among the established divines to whom Fox could turn. He was a
8

prophet, an original, one having authority and not as the scribes...

"For I saw" he wrote, "that there was none among them all that could speak to my condition. And when all my hopes in them and in all men were gone, so that I had nothing outward to help me nor could tell what to do; then, only then, I heard a voice which said, 'There is one, even Christ Jesus, that can speak to thy condition'; and when I heard it my heart did leap for joy."

Fox concluded that he had been forced to eliminate all other sources, so that he could only turn directly to the voice of Christ within – or as he often called it, the Light within. Fox added: "And this I know experimentally" – as we would say, by experience.

Now those words – "There is one, even Christ Jesus that can speak to thy condition; and this I know experimentally" – seem to me the essence. They are for me, anyway. For they record that to be a Quaker is to be a Christian – some Friends would disagree with that; that each of us has his own condition, call it psychological condition if you like, to which God will speak directly and appropriately, if only we could be still and listen...

And when we do hear it, says Fox, there is no doubt about it.

Fox's great theological achievement was to take what you might call "individual inspiration" and so refine it by passing it through the discipline of the group that it did not lead to spiritual anarchy.

It is important to realise that George Fox was a prophet and a mystic, not a philosopher or intellectual. Besides the *Journal* – which was actually an autobiography, dictated retrospectively to be published after his death – he wrote thousands of letters, tracts and epistles, and if you go through them in a scholarly manner, it is possible to maintain that Fox "really meant" a number of things which Quakers do not talk about much today.

To me, it is a bit like trying to figure out what Jesus or Shakespeare "really meant". I do not say it is harmful – it may be helpful – but I think it is difficult and often impossible to know what the first century A.D. or even the 17th century A.D. "really meant". And even if we could know, I am not sure that it would be very useful to us here and now. We are different people, with different modes of speech and thought, products of a very different background. The point is: what canst thou say?

What makes Christ or Fox or Shakespeare great for me today is not that their messages have been permanently deep-frozen for all time, but that their work is so rich, has so many faces and dimensions, that each generation can come to it, find something that is helpful to that generation, and like a successful producer or conductor, make its own new "production", its own re-creation, so that it is new and fresh and compelling once more.

I do not know whether I know exactly what Fox really meant. I only know that there is something in him that speaks to something in me with knockout force.

There are two aspects of what Fox taught which I think make him especially relevant today.

The first is his expedition into the realms of psychology; his realisation that each of us has his own condition, with its weaknesses, struggles and needs – but also the Light within. Fox taught that whoever we had to deal with, we must always address ourselves to that divine spark of goodness.

Consequently, he was singularly uninterested in Sin. He was an optimist; he rejected the Calvinist view of the total depravity of human nature, for a view that asserted freewill and the possibility of salvation for all. He was impatient with Puritan preachers who, as he put it, "roared up for Sin" all the time. Of course men did evil, he said; but keep your eyes on the Light, and evil will not overwhelm you. Because of Christ, our sins are forgiven, so let us drop this unhealthy obsession with the rotten side of human nature.

Some would say that, even today, Friends have rather too rosy a view of human wickedness. Most Friends would admit to having done things they ought not to have done and left undone things they ought to have done. But that there is "no health" in us – or in you – we really cannot accept. And, as any psychologist will tell you, until you can accept yourself as not wholly unlovable, it is impossible to love your neighbour as yourself.

The other point at which Fox's teaching becomes so relevant to today is his non-violence, his peace testimony. He was a big man of striking presence, and the Parliamentary side kept begging him to accept the captaincy of a regiment, to fight against the King. But, said Fox "I told them I was come into the covenant of a Peace which was before wars and strifes were – a witness against all violence..." And so he remained, and so were the Friends who settled among the Indians of North America, and so have Friends in general been ever since.

There is at present a certain seething among Friends about our peace policies. Some think we are no longer strict enough about demanding a peace pledge from every new member. Others think the war against Hitler raised certain aspects of the so-called "Just War" that are not so easily dismissed.

The majority, I think, regard their pacifism as an extremely personal commitment, which they have no right to seek to impose upon others: whatever you must do, I cannot fight. They do not reproach others for failing to share it – nor do they just sit back and say, "I'm a pacifist, you wicked warmongers." Instead, they devote a good deal of effort to trying to establish those communications between antagonists which will promote understanding, and eliminate the causes of violence.

This attitude is encapsulated in a well-known Quaker anecdote about William Penn, a gentleman and a courtier, who continued to wear his sword when he first came among Friends. This sword had once saved his life, and he sought advice from George Fox. Fox counselled: "I advise thee to wear thy sword as long as thou canst." Not long after they met again. "Where is thy sword, William?" enquired Fox. "Oh George," replied William, "I took thy advice, I wore it just as long as I could"

This illustrates what I regard as the two sides of Quaker tolerance at its best. There is nothing to stop a non-pacifist, a sexist or a humanist coming to meeting, except that I fancy after a time he will find the particular sword he wears an increasing embarrassment; until either he decides to take it somewhere else, where it is more in fashion, or he decides to quit wearing it.

One reason for this tendency of Quakers towards a voluntary conformity is that fundamentally we are a Society of Friends. Those who join us do not join "the Society" as number so-and-so; they join a particular meeting (it might be Hampstead or Golders Green, Highgate, Edgware or Muswell Hill). It will probably be a small group of less than a hundred people, and it is to be hoped that these people really will become friends – perhaps people you will love and respect, to whom you can speak frankly, and whom you will not wish to offend unless compelled to by the truth. If you feel you simply do not care for these people as friends, then it may be that the Society is not for you at all.

You will not find here the magical ministrations of an apostolically ordained priest. Nor, oddly enough in this reforming and participatory age, will you find any voting. And yet we like to think of ourselves as the ultimate extension of democracy: when Friends meet to decide whether to call for, say, the banning of pornography – or the painting of our meeting house

13

purple – we will discuss the matter at length, in breadth and in depth.

But, in the end, instead of a show of hands on a motion, the clerk will draft a consensus. And that consensus may well turn out to be something wholly different from any proposal that could have been tabled at the start. For what we are trying to do is not to prove that one party is right and another wrong, but to discover – through periods of silent contemplation as much as noisy argument – what the leading of the spirit is. In the end, it may result in the concern of a single Friend becoming the desire of the unified Society.

It may surprise outsiders to learn that silence is used in business as well as worship meetings. Silent prayer, meditation, goes back far beyond George Fox, of course. But it was rare in the Anglican tradition, which liked to hear everyone saying the same thing at the same time.

Fox was far from being the only perplexed seeker after truth in his day. All over England, and especially in the North, were small groups of men and women looking for a new light to lead them, and certain only that the existing churches could never supply it.

They came to believe that any attempt to impose a structure upon their supplication, or to give authority to any particular minister, would be to impose limits on the Holy Spirit. And so, these "Seekers" as they called themselves, would meet in pure silence, without any programme, and would allow any one of their number who felt that a prayer or prophecy had been entrusted to them to rise and utter it.

14

And these were the people to whom George Fox came, among whom his seed fell and took root – and who gave us this silent, gathered, listening meeting.

The early Friends stood shoulder to shoulder on various beliefs that shocked others around them. There was the lack of interest in Sin; there was the refusal to accept the Bible as ultimate and infallible authority. Fox argued that first of all people must listen to the words of Christ now in their hearts; only after that could they read the Bible with any understanding. The scriptures themselves were dead unless each reader re-experienced and re-wrote them for himself in his own heart.

In a sceptical age, it is perhaps hard for us to realise how revolutionary and outrageous this attitude was – this suggestion that there could be something above Pope, above Church, above Bible, resident in the heart of the ordinary unpriested Christian, and not even administered to him under special conditions. Yet this attitude got Quakers into jail by the thousand.

The early Friends accumulated various other heresies and habits for which they have long since ceased to suffer. Besides refusing to fight, they also refused to address their supposed betters by their titles, or even with the respectful "you" instead of the blunt, old fashioned "thou".

And they refused to take oaths. After all, the apostles, whose church they were trying to restore, had been instructed to let their yea be yea; taking a special oath implied you did not normally tell the truth – and

Quakers made a point of personal integrity which later made them outstanding businessmen.

They also believed in living simply and dressing plainly and abstaining form tobacco and alcohol. To the regret of some, we are less Puritan today. As somebody remarked at a recent Friends' conference – "I never thought the day would come when I could not get near the bar for Quakers...."

Once again these are matters for individual conscience. If Quakers feel they can own a car, take a drink, go to the theatre and laugh on Sundays, it presumably indicates that the atmosphere of the Meeting does not discourage those things. Personally I think it would be bad for us to live too obviously different a way of life from those around us. But I must say, I would rather like to keep my hat on, look the Queen in the eye, and demand briskly "Elizabeth Windsor, how dost thee?"

The importance that Friends attach to their work in the world as expression of their faith is something that speaks increasingly to my condition. I see the essential message of Christ as one of non-violence – a very Quaker message – and I see violence as a form of communication which will impose itself if non-violent methods are not maintained. Thus there can be no more Christian function, surely, than trying to establish communication and understanding between peoples.

Many other Friends have felt called upon to specialise in social service or relief work: you will find them behind many of the big charitable bodies, like Oxfam.

16

Others again act as message-bearers and mediators behind the scenes in Ulster or at the United Nations. Quite a number take on early retirement in order to put their service at the disposal of the Society itself.

But we are a *religious* society, not just a social action group, and to me neither Christ Jesus nor George Fox had a political message to preach. Quakers have no sacraments, no ceremonies, no communion, no-one to administer blessings or baptisms, because we find That of God which is sacramental in the whole of life. The Christ within us – within each of us – is sufficient priest.

I find the silence of Meeting for Worship every Sunday powerful, refreshing and all too short. If you have never attended meeting, you should know that the silence will not usually be total. Three, four or five Friends may rise to utter a brief prayer or deliver some message they find in their hearts, perhaps to read a passage from the gospels – or indeed, anything they feel led to share.

With the help of the spirit, what they will say will weave together into a single rope: a plea for guidance may be answered, a mystery illuminated, a prayer of thanksgiving endorsed. Much depends on the sensitivity of the Friends present. Not every Meeting is rewarding. In some, the contributions may be at cross-purposes, contrived, sentimental or inappropriate. It is a shame when Meeting for Worship becomes a debate.

At the other extreme, there is the silence. And let me assure you – this is something that I find many Catholics know – a long period of total silence can be far from sterile. But it does take some time to get used to it – not to fall asleep, or argue with oneself, or worry about one's income tax. I don't think it has much to do with Oriental meditation, either; nor do Friends have much in common with the Charismatics or Pentecostalists. Perhaps we are just too intellectual – never quite prepared to let go of reason, which is, after all, a very important part of the whole person.

This regard for wholeness also makes us look for manifestations of God in every moment of the life around us, and not just in specially prepared emotional episodes. The silence does take us down, together, to a source of strength and calmness. One of the great values of worshipping together in this way is that the traditions of the Society and the influence and wisdom of Friends do help to protect one from self-deception, arrogance or hysteria. And then one can go out into the world and discover with joy that moments of holiness are waiting round every corner – fragments of God looking out from every face.

I have mentioned that the Society of Friends has no structured order of service, no written creed. If there is a God at all – and that I know experimentally – then we must all see him from our different positions, at different angles, and so all religious talk must be in myths and metaphors – a kind of poetry – and it is folly to attempt to codify it or enforce it, as if one metaphor could have more authority than another.

But Quakerism does have an extensive literature, including a little pamphlet called *Advices and Queries*, which I commend to all enquirers and many forgetful Friends. The Society does not, you see, impose Articles

18

or Commandments upon its members; it simply advises and questions them.

One gets the feeling that instead of commanding "Thou shalt not commit adultery" a Quaker Moses would have asked, embarrassingly; "Do you commit adultery?" Actually I don't think we are over-concerned with your sexual morals; but Friends are supposed to sit quietly from time to time, asking themselves this sort of thing, which – if not quite a creed – does help to create a certain standard.

For example*: Is your religion rooted in personal experience of God?

Do you maintain a steadfast loyalty to Jesus?

Do you keep your mind open to new light and recognise the contribution made by other faiths?

Are you concerned that man's increasing power over nature should be used with reverence for life?

Are you working towards a removal of social injustices and towards a just distribution of the resources of the world?

Do you faithfully maintain our witness against all war?

That's just a partial and potted sample, and I am afraid a good many Friends would have to give some rather muffled answers. Not so much because of their frailties, perhaps, as because we see the Truth as a moving Truth which we must constantly relive and revise in our own hearts.

*These are in the wording of the *Advices & Queries* current when Gerald Priestland wrote the original lecture in 1979.

You will find that Friends on the whole have very little interest on the kind of theological word-games which are not rooted in personal experience, but serve to classify people into groups that are IN and groups that are OUT.

I personally enjoy the company of other Christians – I often find their theology stimulating, and wish them comfort and joy of it all. The point is, they have their condition and I have mine. St Paul's concepts of Redemption and Resurrection do not say anything to me – George Fox's concept of the Light of Christ within everyone says everything; it gives me the trust with which to get up and go on, no matter how many times some appalling piece of news knocks me flat. It may be heretical, but it keeps me happy.

Let me stress that I have been giving you my own understanding of Quakerism, which is by no means the only one. But just as Quakerism must be to many Christians a heresy – a heresy that Friends are delighted to uphold – there are some near-heresies within Quakerism which I find I can cheerfully maintain.

The tradition of love and tolerance between Friends has been remarkably successful in preserving our unity while not discouraging diversity and enquiry. One thing you do not have to leave on the pegs in the Meeting House vestibule is your intellectual integrity. I think I am right in saying that Friends think it is no shame for a member to conclude that his spiritual pilgrimage calls him to move on to some other church which now speaks better to his condition. How could we? So many of us have come here as pilgrims ourselves.

Mind you, all this tolerance could be a way of disguising our spiritual sloppiness and lack of any clear belief. Some of us in the Society have lately been meeting and corresponding in an effort to clarify where Quakerism is going – how it might renew its spiritual springs and its prophetic insights.

As in other churches, we have members urging us to get back to the Good Old Days. We have others saying that the very heart of the Christian message needs a new formulation. And others again who have considerable reservations about the uniqueness of Christ and look increasingly to Oriental religions for the new light.

Whatever our tendencies, I think we are all agreed that we must wait upon the Spirit to see what its will for us may be, and submit such insights as may come to the group, to the Meeting, to the Society as a whole. In a way, we have a new age of Seekers.

So we offer the newcomer the challenge of helping to develop – to cultivate or till, perhaps – a faith that will never be final or complete, that does not claim to have all the answers: one that expresses itself in how you live and work and feel, rather than in what rituals and rigmaroles you adopt; and one for which – when all is said and done – simple, honest people were prepared to suffer and die not so long ago.

It is not a faith to rush into. If you feel that it does speak to your condition, my advice would be to come to meetings as an uncommitted attender for at least a year, before you take the step of writing to the Clerk of Monthly Meeting, asking to be accepted into membership; then you will be called on by a couple of visitors – at least one of whom will be familiar to you – who will satisfy themselves that you really know what you are doing.

What do you lose? Well, as much time and money for the Society as you feel you can spare. And I must confess I do miss a good lusty hymn from time to time. But when I think of the gains – nobody singing off key, no fatuous sermons, no barbarous canticles or dubious professions of faith – then such liberty is well worth the price.

And there are more positive gains. Friendship, I hope; the challenge I have spoken of; and the right to retain your intellectual self-respect; the right to be a happy heretic and not get burnt; the sense of coming home to a place you were always meant to be – for as we say, Quakers are "convinced" not converted.

George Fox said he came to it "experimentally" – and as I said, we should say "by experience". But don't hesitate to try us as an experiment. Who knows, the experiment may lead to experience; but that is something only you can prove. We have no secret mantra, no laying-on of hands, no magic dip. Only the silence in which you may hear that still small voice that has been within you, waiting to speak to you, all the time.

FURTHER READING

Richard Allen, *Yours in Friendship*, (QHS 1995)

— *Silence and Speech*, (QHS 1998)

Britain Yearly Meeting of the Religious Society of Friends; *Quaker faith and practice*, BYM 1995

— *Advices and Queries*, BYM 1995

Alastair Heron, *The British Quakers 1647-1997: highlights of their history*, (Curlew 1997)

Harvey Gillman, *A Light that is Shining*, (Quaker Books 2003)

George H. Gorman, *The Amazing fact of Quaker Worship*, (QHS 1979)

Pierre Lacout, *God is Silence*, (Quaker Books reprint 2001)

John Punshon, *Portrait in Grey: A short history of the Quakers*, (QHS 1991)

Jack H. Wallis, *Jung and the Quaker Way*, (QHS 1992)

These and many other Quaker and Quaker related books are available from The Quaker Bookshop, Friends House, 173-177 Euston Road, London NW1 2BJ, phone 020 7663 1030, e-mail: bookshop@quaker.org.uk or visit the website www.quaker.org.uk. A full list of Quaker literature will be sent on request. Further information about the Religious Society of Friends (Quakers) will be sent on request to Quaker Life Outreach Section at the above address, phone 020 7663 1025, email: carmelk@quaker.org.uk